R. D. HOLLOWAY

Grand- and Great- Wisdom

Life Lessons from My Grandparents, Great-Aunts and Great-Uncles

First edition

This book was professionally typeset on Reedsy.
Find out more at reedsy.com

*In loving memory of all my grandparents,
great-aunts and great-uncles,
including those I never met.*

Everyone needs to have access both to grandparents and grandchildren in order to be a full human being.

— MARGARET MEAD
ANTHROPOLOGIST

NOBODY CAN DO FOR LITTLE CHILDREN WHAT GRANDPARENTS DO. GRANDPARENTS SORT OF SPRINKLE STARDUST OVER THE LIVES OF LITTLE CHILDREN.

— ALEX HALEY
NOVELIST

Contents

1

Introduction

Having a multi-generational family is a blessing for those wanting to live their best life. It's the perfect way to learn how to make good choices.

Listening to sage advice from your elders is not the only way to discern lessons, either.

It does not take long, even as a child, to think, "Ooh, I don't want to be like Great-Aunt Betsy" or "Gosh, Uncle Harry is just the best!"

It's easy to see how life-long behavior, attitude, and character traits have shaped the lives of older family members. With luck, they have lived long enough to recognize and apply the lessons that each challenging or joyful experience teaches.

When considering the benefits their insights can offer, there is no wonder elders are revered in so many cultures, from Ancient Rome to Greece, Korea, India, most Oriental and African cultures, and among Native Americans.[1,2]

If you have moved into the "older generation" of your family, take some time to ponder your triumphs, your mistakes, and the stories you want to be remembered. Even if the younger members of your family seem not to have interest now, that could change.

If you are one of those younger family members, take advantage of your "walking encyclopedias" while you can. The wisdom and tales they can offer is so much richer than anything you can find on a website. A computer can't hug you, and giggle or cry with you. So, why not learn from their experience or by their example?

Observe your elders, but without judging. After all, no one is perfect. Without asking, you cannot know what factors influenced their life decisions.

Decide which of them you admire and trust. Talk with them about their lives.

If you have a problem, ask them how they faced a similar situation. They might or might not have some advice. If they messed it up, at least you will have an idea of what not to do.

Just because there weren't "x" and "z" technologies or "y" values when they were growing up, doesn't mean your older family members can't understand what is bothering you now. Personal interactions change very little through the years. That's how the principles of psychology, propaganda, and advertising have stayed basically the same for decades.

I've traveled much of the world, talking with people of all ages and many cultures. Everyone I met wanted basically the same things: to feel loved, to feel accepted by a group, to be heard, and to feel valued. That applies no matter your age or situation.

My own childhood experience in a large family is an example of how older family members, even without realizing it, teach the youngsters in their family. These are the eight elders who had the greatest impact on me and whose influences still shape my life.

As for readers who are children and teens, as I was at the time, perhaps my experience can show you how to learn from your elders by the way they treat you and each other.

Large or small, family dynamics are much the same. If you don't have older generations around, then family friends, or neighbors you trust, can substitute. The same goes for older folks who don't have youngsters around. Volunteering for groups from the other generation is another way to share, either direction.

My family just happened to have large numbers of siblings in every branch of my grandparents' generation. The middle generation loved it. By promoting good relations between their parents and their children, my parents were able to take a two-week childfree break every summer. After one week, my sister and I would be swapped between the grandparents so that each of us got one week of focused love and attention from one set of grandparents.

So isn't that a great reason to promote family harmony for everyone involved?

I certainly thought it was. Not to mention the fabulous cookies involved, each branch of the family was full of vivid characters who populate the movie script of my childhood memories.

Before continuing, you deserve some background.

My family comes from the Deep South, and I write of them through the filter of their culture during the 1950s and 60s. It was a time of great tension and change.[3,4] When not visiting there, I lived outside that culture and thus was perplexed by their ways. It created my tendency to observe without commenting.

With the passing of years and my parents' patient answers, I gained context and insight into the slow way that cultures change their concept of fairness and equality. By talking frankly with my grands and greats, I learned when to set aside my battle gear and love them with their flaws. Many were brave. Others were not.

For example, in the world of my grandmothers, few women could excel outside the realm of the domestic arts.[5] With such limited intellectual confines, it's no wonder conversations with some family members and their friends were tainted with spiteful envy and petty gossip. I vowed not to follow them into that trap, and tried to introduce more positive topics.

Fortunately, I saw little of such shortcomings openly exhibited by my family elders. Maybe they were on their best behavior when I was around, since I had made my views obvious as I matured. If so, I am grateful for their restraint.

Unfailingly, they all showed me great love, as best they could, which is what all children really need.

There is one Southernism that I should clarify. I doubt it's unique to my family, but perhaps times are changing what was then considered a nicety. I've seen a similar practice in other countries.

Kids my age often called their aunts and uncles by their first name, no title. Great-aunts and great-uncles were called aunts and uncles. That's why my great-aunt, Irene, goes by the name of Aunt Irene in this book.

I write about my family in a generic sense here, without last names or locations. Relatives who receive this book will know who they are, and I ask you to understand that I present them as I knew them growing up. I acknowledge that your view may be very different.

My intention is to lovingly offer these grands and greats to all of you, readers, as exemplars you might recognize in relatives from your own youth, whether that was decades ago or you are living it now.

May you find them familiar enough to discern new life lessons from your own family.

2

Mama

My Mother's Mother

W*hat I learned from her: kindness, love, acceptance, common sense, determination, humility, story-telling, cooking*

My mother called her mother "Mama," with a Southern

accent. It came out MAH-muh. To our childish ears, it sounded like Mommer, so that's what she became to my sister and me. We would never have dared to write it that way after the first grade, however.

Mama was a woman of medium height, with a lovely patrician face, wavy hair, and kind, knowing brown eyes. She was the gentlest person I have ever met.

This was a woman who knew hard times.

One of 10 children, eight of them girls, she was a farmer's daughter. She and her sisters helped her parents pick cotton in the field. Their mother, who must have been an accomplished homemaker, taught them cooking and needle arts. It seemed each girl had one or two specialties in each.

Mama married at 15 and had her first child at 16, a little boy. After that, tragedies struck as she had miscarriages and what she called a "blue baby." At last, nearly 15 years later, she got her little girl, my mother.

Mama's husband, one of five siblings, was a timber estimator by profession and a barterer by nature. I often heard it said that he could leave the house in the morning with a pocketknife and come home in the evening with a horse. He provided well enough for his family in spite of the Great Depression. They had a modest, comfortable home in a middling sized town on the Mississippi River, only half a block from the levee. When he took sick, an extra room, where he could sleep without disturbing anyone, was built off the back porch. He died at age 52, leaving my grandmother a widow long before I was born. Only three years later, her son died tragically.

Somehow, Mama carried on after such terrible blows. My mother was two years into college and already engaged (or nearly) to my father. She dropped out and went home for about a year before marrying my father in 1944, just as he began serving in the U.S. Navy. Mom stayed at home until my father came back from the war, which I'm sure helped Mama adjust.

When my parents began their life elsewhere, Mama kept her life in order with some savvy decisions. As needed, she would rent out that little room off the porch for "pin money." One side of her property ran along a major highway through town and when times got tough, she sold a small corner as a used car lot. Even scraping by, she kept her surroundings beautiful.

Visiting Mama in the summers was better than Christmas. My mind's eye can see her in the kitchen teaching me to listen to the sizzle to tell when chicken was fried just right, or standing at her white enameled kitchen work table stirring cookie batter in a cornflower blue pottery mixing bowl. I still have her recipes for tea cakes and sugar cookies.

After meals, I would explore the huge and intriguing yard, swing high as I could on the metal pipe swing set, and attempt to pull myself up on metal rings hanging in the middle. My grandfather really had brought home a horse for my mother and had built a stable for it. The stable became a storage shed, where I could spend hours spying into boxes of old toys. If I got peckish, I could grab a pomegranate from the huge bush by the front door, taking care not to cut myself on the whipsaw thin leaves.

One feature I remember best was the goldfish pond. Shaded by tall lush trees, the pond was edged with sitting stones and accented by elephant ears. When I was really small and my parents were visiting, too, I got restless during the requisite post-lunch nap. Grabbing a cane fishing pole, without any idea of how to fish, I started dragging the hook across the water. One of the biggest fish in that pond jumped up and bit the hook, almost pulling the pole out of my hands. I managed to lift it up but had no idea what to do. Terrified that I would kill it, I began hollering for help. Everyone came running. Mama and my mother laughed so hard that they were holding their sides. My father recovered first and gently freed the poor creature back into the water.

Inside Mama's house, I remember everything, but loved the breezeway best. Where the porch reached over to the extra room there were about eight feet that had a roof and screened walls not blocked by either building. When it was muggy and really hot, which was most of the summer, that was the place to gather.

Mama had fixed it up with a metal glider sofa with soft upholstered cushions, a coffee table big enough to put up your feet or play games, and several types of wicker chairs with matching cushions she had made. Her big gray Westinghouse hassock fan kept the air stirring on still days, whether pointing at us or on its back cooling our propped feet.

The reason I write so much about Mama is that she came to live with us after breaking her hip in a fall. Before that, she also had come to share my room to nurse me through many bouts of allergy-induced pneumonia. I loved having her there. She would tell me stories of her family: what it was like to pick cotton, ride in a horse-drawn wagon into town, cook with a wood stove, or how exciting her first rides in trains and cars had been. We talked about everything from changes like the telephone and television, to equal rights and religion. I could ask her anything.

After coming to stay, Mama earned her keep. Her particular skill was sewing. She could walk into a store, look at a dress, go buy supplies, and make a flawless copy that fit like a glove. She easily could have been a designer or a tailor. Mama even upholstered furniture and made exquisite Barbie doll dresses for my presents.

Besides making our clothes, Mama took over the kitchen whenever my mother was working. The two of them set up a kind of cooking school for my sister and me. She taught us such baking skills that by age nine I had made a perfect lemon meringue pie. We always had cakes and cookies at the ready for my father and visiting neighbors.

After my father took his dream job in a small town, we moved into a place where Mama had her own "suite" next to the kitchen, so she didn't have to climb stairs. After school, I would come to her room to play our favorite games, like dominoes.

We kept Mama with us for as long as we could, even when she could barely get out of bed. She had a caregiver during school hours and I would take over until my parents got home from work and fixed supper. We would watch her favorite television shows and talk about our days. Mama always had a story ready to tell. I learned my passions for communicating, family history, cooking, and needle crafts from her.

Eventually, Mama left us, as each generation must do. I still feel sad that she's gone, but only for a moment. What vibrant memories we created with few worldly goods. How much she taught me about life. Her gentleness and love stay with me always, a standard I try to maintain.

3

Aunt Irene

My Mother's Aunt

What I learned from her: industry, gumption, sincerity, competition, skepticism, pragmatism, genealogy, crochet

Aunt Irene was one of Mama's sisters, some seven years younger, who lived a block and half down the street. She was cafeteria director for the school across from her house, and a talented cook. She could masterfully quilt, crochet, or needlepoint, as well as knit or sew.

I have a photo of all the sisters in their youth. Irene's skin is tanned by the sun and her dark hair frames her face with a regal crown of braids, making her beauty stand out even among her pretty sisters. When Aunt Irene sneaked off to a dance at the next town over, her future husband started courting her immediately. She married at age 17.

Early on, the couple had a gas station. She prepared snacks to sell to regular customers and hungry travelers. They owned the house next to theirs, with four two-rut driveways in between. With their usual business acumen, that house remained rented to supplement their income. At the back of the driveways, they built a single, long, open-front, tin-roofed shed as a kind of carport for protection and storage.

Whenever there was a family gathering, usually a funeral or wedding, Aunt Irene held a reunion catfish fry in the driveway area. It was the perfect setting, with lots of room and shade for serving tables and groupings of chairs. Even better, the school playground across the street was fenced but had an opening so that neighborhood kids could play anytime. My cousins and I would run over there and spend hours playing in a safe, easily supervised environment. During my summer visits, as well, I took full advantage of the merry-go-round, jungle gym, monkey bars and slides.

Aunt Irene would set up a huge vat for frying and produced the lightest, crispiest catfish, which became my gold standard for comparison. All of the sisters, in-laws, and cousins pitched in with their specialty dishes and cold drinks, lending a hand with the work, too. Cousins would catch up on each other's lives, family stories were recounted, and there always was lots of laughter and, sometimes, nostalgic tears.

Aunt Irene and her husband shared a focus on staying busy, whether in work or play. Aunt Irene was rarely defeated at Scrabble, having memorized all of the x, z, q, and two-letter words in the Scrabble dictionary. Her keen mind and curiosity were evident in every project she undertook.

Spending time with her was easy and she taught me so much. With patience, she had me eager to compete with her at Scrabble at almost every visit. She taught me how to crochet, which I still enjoy. I was less enthusiastic about needlepoint, but have several pretty pillows from that era. When she cooked for me, there always were lessons and tips involved that I still use.

We had lively conversations as we worked. Aunt Irene was forthright in her opinions. For example, she went to church every Sunday that she could, asking for rides even after she could no longer drive. I will never forget one Sunday afternoon, as we were talking, a noted evangelist came on the television and I was surprised when she got up to turn it off.

She turned to me and said, "I have never given one penny to a TV evangelist and I never will." It enraged her that money kept being asked from folks who worked hard to earn their pennies while that person flew around the country in a private jet, among other things that did not fit her idea of how a man of the cloth should behave.

Aunt Irene was just as passionate about maintaining the family history, and in an active way. She was the keeper of family photographs, with shoe boxes full. Proudly she showed me how she had traced an old photo of a family reunion from when her parents were in their prime and my mother was just a child. She had numbered each figure and typed a corresponding list of their names to the side, after checking with remaining sisters and cousins for the few names she couldn't remember. Then she had mimeographed the drawing for family, and it became a much-photocopied reference work for the generations. It's no wonder I love genealogy.

Some visits, I would just pull out that picture and ask questions about the cousins I didn't know. Her mind really was like an encyclopedia until she died at the age of 95.

After Mama died, Aunt Irene turned into my "adopted" grandmother. I visited her as often as I could make the drive.

My respect for her grew as I watched her put her talents to use to add to her Social Security benefits. By the hundreds, she crocheted doilies, napkins, and tablecloths, or cut and finished quilts, or knitted sweaters. Through a network she had created at all the local fabric and yarn shops, she constantly worked on commissioned projects. I have no doubts that, had the internet been available, Aunt Irene would have had her own website.

As I took her to doctor visits, her courage in facing her physical challenges filled me with awe and inspiration. Even now, I think of her indomitable attitude when difficulties arise.

What shocked me most, and filled me with wonder, was the way she faced down life's final hurdle. On one visit, she stared at me until I was focused on her and asked me to go with her to the funeral home. Calmly, and with great practicality, she explained that she already had made all the arrangements she could by phone. After catching my breath, I took her. She walked among the caskets, asking my opinion, and finally chose one that suited her. We sat with the funeral director as she confirmed instructions and paid the bill.

Afterward, I took her out to eat at her favorite cafeteria. As we ate, Aunt Irene kept the mood light while discussing her arrangements. Her humor and pragmatism were brilliant.

4

Uncle Charlie

Aunt Irene's Husband

W*hat I learned from him:* *patience, joy, teaching with inspiration, savoring the moment, fishing, checkers*

Even though he died when I was not yet 12, Uncle Charlie was like a treasured grandfather to me. He assumed that role since Mama's husband had died more than a decade before my birth.

I adored Uncle Charlie. He was funny and kind, with a generous nature. I was drawn to his twinkling eyes, humor, and zest for living. An average man in stature and looks, Uncle Charlie was memorable for his easy smile, amiable behavior, and his perpetual favorite hat.

By the time I knew him, the gas station was no more. His time in World War I or as a contractor "out west" with Aunt Irene were rarely mentioned. Their two sons were grown.

He rented a large and lush tract of land on the edge of town with tall trees and a fishing pond, where he kept cattle and horses. It was only as an adult that I realized the property had belonged to my grandfather and the rent was paid to Mama, which benefited them both.

Uncle Charlie often took me out there with him, a treat that thrilled me and made me feel so grown up. As he fed the stock, he sometimes talked about his favorite horse, Chesterfield. Aunt Irene kept pictures of him training and riding that big white gelding.

Even better, Uncle Charlie taught me to fish at that pond. He must have heard the story about my nap-time antics. I was very young, but so eager. We would walk together through the trees with our cane poles. With patience and good humor, he taught me how to bait a hook with a worm, keep still watching for the float to bob, then set the hook and pull in the fish. It's a pastime I still love, even when I don't catch a thing.

Uncle Charlie's game was checkers, and he was just as accomplished at it as Aunt Irene was at Scrabble. I wanted so badly to learn, but I really was too young for this, too. He showed me the basics anyway and would play a game with me willingly, gently pointing out potential mistakes. He probably enjoyed my excitement when I would win.

Eventually, I caught on that Uncle Charlie was letting me win often enough to keep me enthusiastic. Since by then I was old enough to understand, he promised not to do it anymore and upped his level of instruction. I took the challenge and we became happy adversaries over the checkerboard.

In retrospect, Uncle Charlie could have been so different after fighting in WWI and after he and Aunt Irene lost their three-month-old daughter. He even smiled and tried to cheer me up during a hospital visit after part of his leg had been surgically removed. Although that memory is hard, I am glad I was allowed to visit and show him how important he was in my life.

5

Grandmother

My Father's Mother

W*hat I learned from her:* *graciousness, pride, precision, mystery, self-awareness, dedication, pickles*

Grandmother was from the smallest branch of my family tree, being one of only four children. As she rarely came to visit us, I saw her mostly in the summers of my one-week visits.

Grandmother attended college, a rarity in those times. She worked as a teller at the local bank, with a professional and amiable presence. Folks around town never failed to greet her when we went on errands.

I remember Grandmother being tall and somewhat gaunt, with an inner tension that perplexed me. Outside of work, she seemed uncomfortable around people to me. Nevertheless, she showed gentle humor at the dinner table.

Although Grandmother did not like to talk about herself, as a sociable child, I was persistent and probably a pest. I loved her and wanted to know more about her.

As she seemed always to be working in the kitchen, that's where I would attempt to draw her out. She would talk to me about her family and its long history in the area.

Her favorite subject, though, was cooking.

Grandmother's fried chicken and her pot roast were exceptional. When the "menfolk" went hunting, she never failed to cook up something delectable from the dove or venison. Her prowess in almost every food category was remarkable. She knew just how to bring out the best flavor in the corn, tomatoes, okra, butter beans and other fresh vegetables from the garden. I watched in fascination when she made preserves with figs fresh from her trees.

To me, though, her bread and butter pickles were perfection itself. I could have eaten them with anything. My parents raved about her piccalilli, but it was beyond my child's palate.

In my twenties, I managed to get Grandmother to share with me her recipe for bread and butter pickles. This was a major accomplishment, since her recipes were a jealously guarded secret. This still makes me chuckle, recalling that she, as did so many other accomplished Southern cooks, left out her secret ingredient. I still don't know what it was.

Grandmother did have a delightful passion. On Friday nights in autumn, she would accompany her husband to the high school football games. The stadium was just outside their back gate, so they would walk together with their stadium seats and blankets to cheer on the local team. I heard that the land had once been theirs and they got lifetime entry to the games in their deal with the school district.

6

Granddaddy

My Father's Father

W *hat I learned from him: respect, faith, tolerance, compassion, persistence, integrity, contentment, playfulness, joy*

Granddaddy remains one of my favorite human beings.

I remember squealing in delight as a tot when he pretended to pinch off my nose with the knuckles of two fingers, then said "gotcha" as he showed me the knuckles with the tip of his thumb protruding from them. He always had time to play, toss me up in the air, or tickle me.

Granddaddy was one of 10 siblings who grew up on a dirt road through the woods. He and three of his brothers had studied shape-note music and performed as a quartet at churches in their early years. One of his pleasures was serving as choirmaster at church, which he did for decades. Often as not he would be listening to the radio and humming along.

Early on, Granddaddy owned the dry goods store in town. He had just expanded to the small town next door when the Great Depression hit in late 1929. Granddaddy kept his stores open as long as he could but was forced to close them both. When telling me about those days, he taught me valuable lessons about the way he saw life. With sadness, he would look me straight in the eyes so I would pay attention.

As he told it, Granddaddy set up store accounts for both white and Black folks. That was not common practice in the South at that time, and he took flak for it. He told me that most of his white customers shrugged off their debt. With emphasis and respect, he said that nearly all of his Black customers continued to repay him as best they could, even if all they could do was leave fresh eggs, fruit, or vegetables at his kitchen door. Even as I teen, I would still see offerings there.

Granddaddy later worked as the town water superintendent. When he retired, he went to work at the local dry goods store for the new owners. I loved visiting him at that huge, wood-paneled store, gazing at the shelves that went all the way to the high ceiling. My eyes always went to the ornate and colorful teacups. Granddaddy would bring down to the counter the ones I thought were prettiest so I could look at them better. Somehow, on many birthdays or Christmases, one of them would end up among my gifts.

Granddaddy must have acquired several lots around their house. The back and one side of the yard were full of tall trees, mostly pecans. There were fig trees in the backyard, too, and there always was a respectable vegetable garden around one corner. The other side was more open all the way to the cross street. I would play with some kids my age and imagine all sorts of tales as we ran in this and others yards through the neighborhood. When I first saw the movie "To Kill a Mockingbird," I knew exactly what Harper Lee was depicting.

I wish I had inherited Granddaddy's green thumb. One year he decided that their garden was not sufficient. He found a tractor and plowed up the lot along the cross road. It was a magnificent project, protected by deer fencing, and full of corn stalks and verdant plants of tomatoes, purple hull peas, butter beans,okra, and more. Paired with Grandmother's skill in the kitchen, we ate like royalty on produce filled with flavor and goodness not to be found in a grocery store now. I have no doubt that Granddaddy shared this abundance where needed.

One of the sweetest memories of my grandparents, though, is the deep peace at the closing of the day. Their house had a large, roofed front porch, open on the sides and raised up about five steps from the yard. It had majestic ceiling fans and comfortable wicker rocking chairs looking out across the street.

Most summer evenings, my grandparents would sit out there in their rockers while I chased lightning bugs in the front yard. As the sun would fade and the fans gained purchase on the currents of steamy air, you could almost believe there was a breeze. About that point, Granddaddy would start humming. Then he would sing his favorite hymns, like "How Great Thou Art." Wandering toward the music, I would settle on the top step and soak in the beauty of the moment.

7

Auntie

My Father's Aunt

W *hat I learned from her: passion, advocacy, adventure, desire to learn, hilarity, gentle rebellion, travel, panache*

Auntie was a trailblazer and irrepressible character. Her accomplishments set the bar high for any contemporary women of the Deep South, as well as for me. She was an outspoken college graduate who brooked no bigotry, by her definition of the term.

Grandmother's older sister, Auntie lived in the old family home two blocks up the street. She was a career woman, first as a teacher and the town's first female school board member.

She then took on setting up the town's first state welfare office, eventually directing the state's social work program for what would be an eight-county region. That meant she had to drive to all parts of the area by herself from the 1930s until she retired. She did so without fear, although she did tell me that she kept a pistol tucked away at her husband's insistence.

Auntie was a deep thinker, political activist and liberal in a conservative community. Her work was recognized by the governor and admired even by those who disagreed with her.

Every month, Auntie played Booray with her friends, including a pair of neighboring sisters who were Jewish. She was a voracious reader and a strong woman with plenty of verve. She died at 95.

In spite of working, Auntie also excelled in some of the domestic arts. Every year, she would make from scratch dozens of unforgettably delicious and huge tamales from the venison her husband brought back from his hunting trips. She always had a needlework project handy.

Auntie cherished her home and its history, telling fascinating stories about it and our family. I'm still not sure if Jesse James really did leave his horse in her father's care once. Of course, part of the reason her house stayed so beautiful was the contribution of her cook and housekeeper, a Black woman who shared her first name. They had been together for decades, and it tickled me how they would joke and grouse with each other like family.

I loved to visit Auntie, especially in the evenings as I got older. Conversation always was delightful as we would peruse the names and dates recorded in the family Bible, or she would tell me the history of treasured items in the house. It seemed each book, piece of crystal, or table just waited for her to recount how it came to be there.

Auntie talked of her travels and knew everything about her town and its history. Even her Siamese cat required a conversational sidebar when it emerged from under the furniture.

Once I was in college, our conversations included some sipping bourbon in the evenings. With a grin, she would give me cloves to chew before I walked home, in hopes that my abstinent grandparents would not catch on.

8

Uncle Frank

Auntie's Husband

W*hat I learned from him: respect for hunters, appreciation of the outdoors, compassion for limitations, caution*

UNCLE FRANK

Uncle Frank had the car dealership in town and supported Auntie well. They never had children, but were devoted to each other.

Although Uncle Frank died when I was 13, I remember him as a lithe and dapper man with a neat brush mustache, usually wearing a panama hat. He was funny and light-hearted, always to be found outside with his hounds when not in the house.

Uncle Frank fascinated me. He looked like a city slicker, but loved to hunt and carefully cared for his pack of hunting dogs. He always brought home meat for the table, usually venison.

I had not been exposed to hunting and hated the idea of killing wild animals. But Uncle Frank showed me to respect the viewpoint of hunters who did so without needless slaughter, to provide food for their family and friends.

A particular object of my fascination was his hunting horn. He had made a loud horn out of a large beautiful conch shell. When I tried, I never could get a sound out of it.

A burden Auntie and Uncle Frank both bore was increasing deafness. It made for some interesting conversations. They fussed over misunderstandings, but humor would prevail.

One day, Uncle Frank loaded up his truck with his hounds and took off with his dog handler on a hunting trip. He crossed a raised train track with a non-functioning warning. I imagine he never heard the train over the hounds' barking. Such accidents were not uncommon in the Deep South in those days. I still wish I could have known Uncle Frank better.

9

My other Uncle Frank

My Father's Uncle

*W*hat I learned from him: *family diplomacy, helpfulness, respect for repair technicians, antiques*

This Uncle Frank was "baby brother" to Grandmother and Auntie. Although I saw him at family gatherings, I didn't get to know him until my teens and twenties. But I heard about him.

He was brilliant, an electrical engineer with Boeing, and could fix just about anything. I became increasingly impressed by Uncle Frank's willingness to make frequent trips to help his widowed sisters maintain their houses. I believe this showed him to have a generous heart.

Uncle Frank and his wife were fervent antique hunters and led their own interesting life. Like Auntie, they had a story about each special item in their home.

As sometimes happens in families, I came to understand that his sisters and his wife did not get along. Their tiffs could be amusing, but mostly I remember feeling dismay and pity as Uncle Frank practiced hopeful diplomacy.

At rare times, I saw him standing among them and raising his voice. I never was sure if it was to overcome deafness or to halt hostilities, whether overt or velvet-gloved.

Fortunately for everyone's tranquility, Uncle Frank lived almost 400 miles away so there usually was an excuse to come alone on his visits.

10

Conclusion

Why do I think it's so important for children and older family members to get to know each other and interact with true interest and trust?

The answer goes far beyond the obvious benefits mentioned in my introduction.

Today's overloaded schedules and self-involved habits of online games, web surfing and binge watching make it so easy to forget about the importance of interacting with people on a face-to-face basis.

We are social animals, programmed to develop social skills in the context of family and community. We need the physical presence of people we trust in order to thrive, especially the simple acts of conversation and touch. This is particularly true for both children and seniors.[6]

Concerns that overuse of social media is undermining the ability to relate in family and community structures are serious.[7] Additional isolation in the recent pandemic made it harder for children and adults alike to maintain meaningful contact.

Parents in the middle need to encourage their parents and their children to interact. A little patience and savvy hints might work wonders.

Mentioning to a child something interesting that their grandparent has done might spark a conversation between the two later on. It's a vital part of development for children and teens to see their family members not as a label, but as interesting and multi-dimensional people.

Interacting with and nurturing children has an equally healthy effect on members of the older generation.[6] Being around youthful enthusiasm can uplift spirits and brighten outlooks.

Perhaps describing how my beloved elders guided me to grow along positive pathways will help both youngsters, as I was then, and elders, as I am now, to recognize each other in my stories.

Just observing how the other generation interacts with their circumstances can be positive and instructive. There is reciprocal wisdom in both maturity and youth.

Reinforcing bonds between generations in a family can teach, heal and expand hearts.

Applying those same lessons in our communities might eventually heal the world.

CONCLUSION

If you have enjoyed reading "Grand- and Great- Wisdom," I would appreciate it if you could leave a favorable review on Amazon!

11

Resources

1. (2017b, December 7). *7 Cultures That Celebrate Aging And Respect Their Elders*. HuffPost. Retrieved October 10, 2022, from https://www.huffpost.com/entry/what-other-cultures-can-teach_n_483 4228
2. Moorhouse, P. (2020b, February 24). *THE CULTURES WHERE ELDERS ARE REVERED*. Retrieved October 10, 2022, from https://www.linkedin.com/pulse/cultures-where-elders-revered-pam-moorhouse
3. History.com Editors. (2022, May 11). *The 1950s*. HISTORY. Retrieved October 10, 2022, from https://www.history.com/topics/cold-war/1950s
4. *Race Relations in the 1930s and 1940s | Great Depression and World War II, 1929-1945 | U.S. History Primary Source Timeline | Classroom Materials at the Library of Congress | Library of Congress*. (n.d.). The Library of Congress. Retrieved October 10, 2022, from https://www.loc.gov/classroom-materials/united-states-history-primary-source-timeline/great-depression-and-world-war-ii-1929-1945/race-relations-in-1930s-and-1940s/

5. American Experience. (2018, March 13). *Mrs. America: Women's Roles in the 1950s*. American Experience | PBS. Retrieved October 10, 2022, from https://www.pbs.org/wgbh/americanexperience/features/pill-mrs-america-womens-roles-1950s/

6. Menges, S. (2022, May 18). *The 3 Biggest Advantages of Human Touch May Surprise You*. PlushCare. Retrieved October 10, 2022, from https://plushcare.com/blog/advantages-of-human-touch-hugs/

7. Ekern, M. J. S. (2021, April 20). Social Media Addiction in Families: What is the Impact? *Addiction Hope*. Retrieved October 10, 2022, from https://www.addictionhope.com/blog/social-media-addiction-families/

Made in the USA
Middletown, DE
18 October 2022

13051846R00031